this 3D book belongs to:

TIME INC. BOOKS

Publisher Margot Schupf
Vice President, Finance Terri Lombardi
Executive Director, Marketing Services Carol Pittard
Executive Director, Business Development Suzanne Albert
Executive Director, Marketing Susan Hettleman
Executive Publishing Director Megan Pearlman
Associate Director of Publicity Courtney Greenhalgh
Assistant General Counsel Simone Procas
Assistant Director, Special Sales Ilene Schreider
Assistant Director, Finance Christine Font
Assistant Production Director Susan Chodakiewicz
Senior Manager, Sales Marketing Danielle Costa
Senior Manager, Children's Category Marketing Amanda Lipnick
Manager, Business Development and Partnerships Stephanie Braga
Associate Production Manager Amy Mangus
Associate Prepress Manager Alex Voznesenskiy

Editorial Director Stephen Koepp
Art Director Gary Stewart
Senior Editors Roe D'Angelo, Alyssa Smith
Managing Editor Matt DeMazza
Editor, Children's Books Jonathan White
Copy Chief Rina Bander
Design Manager Anne-Michelle Gallero
Assistant Managing Editor Gina Scauzillo
Editorial Assistant Courtney Mifsud

Special thanks: Allyson Angle, Keith Aurelio, Katherine Barnet, Brad Beatson, Jeremy Biloon, Ian Chin, Rose Cirrincione, Pat Datta, Assu Etsubneh, Alison Foster, Erika Hawxhurst, Kristina Jutzi, David Kahn, Jean Kennedy, Hillary Leary, Samantha Long, Kimberly Marshall, Robert Martells, Nina Mistry, Melissa Presti, Danielle Prielipp, Kate Roncinske, Babette Ross, Dave Rozzelle, Matthew Ryan, Ricardo Santiago, Divyam Shrivastava

TIME For Kids
Editor Nellie Gonzalez Cutler

Stereographer David E. Klutho
3D Graphics Designer ron labbe, studio 3D
3D Photography Assistant Jake Huber
Writer Curtis Slepian
Production Coordinator Laura Henning Vandeven
Photography Editor Marguerite Schropp Lucarelli
Editorial Production Manager Raphael Joa

This book is dedicated to Austin, Ally, Aaron and NGO

Special thanks: Victor and Joan Klutho, John A. Kilo, Keippi and Dexter Cobble, Laciny Brothers, Canon USA, Nikon USA, Panasonic Lumix 3D, and Sony 3D

For information on TIME For Kids magazine for the classroom or home, go to timeforkids.com or call 800-777-8600.
For subscriptions to TIME For Kids, go to timeforkids.com or call 877-604-8017.

Published by TIME For Kids Books,
An imprint of Time Inc. Books
1271 Avenue of the Americas, 6th floor
New York, NY 10020

ISBN 10: 1-61893-145-8
ISBN 13: 978-1-61893-145-0
Library of Congress Control Number: 2015938279

TIME For Kids is a trademark of Time Inc.

We welcome your comments and suggestions about TIME For Kids Books. Please write to us at:

TIME For Kids Books, Attention: Book Editors, P.O. Box 361095, Des Moines, IA 50336-1095
If you would like to order any of our hardcover Collector's Edition books, please call us at 800-327-6388, Monday through Friday, 7 a.m.–9 p.m. Central Time.

1 TLF 15

We gratefully acknowledge and thank the folllowing persons and places for allowing us to photograph their animals that appear in this book:

Blue Skyy Stables (Missouri)
Butler University
Butterfly Wonderland (Arizona)
Butterfly World (Florida)
Cabela's
Cincinnati Zoo
Cleveland Metro Parks Zoo
Denver Zoo
Eoff Ranch, Clinton, Arkansas
Indianapolis Zoo
Lion Country Safari
Little Rock Zoo
Louisville Zoo
Memphis Zoo
Miami Seaquarium
Milwaukee County Zoo
Nashville Zoo
Omaha Henry Doorly Zoo
Phoenix Zoo
Pittsburgh Zoo
Ringling Bros. and Barnum & Bailey Circus
Purina Pro Plan Incredible Dog Challenge
Professional Bull Riders
Saint Louis Zoo
St. Louis Disc Dogs
United States Air Force Academy
University of Colorado
University of Texas
Wild Animal Safari (Missouri)
Wildlife World Zoo (Arizona)
World Bird Sanctuary
Zoo Miami

READY FOR A TREAT?
PUT ON YOUR 3D GLASSES NOW!
TIME
Animal ADVENTURES 3D

JUMPING FOREWORD
with GRACE BUSCH

This is my horse, Rebel, but his show name is Casanova. That's the name he goes by in competitions. Rebel is an amazing 7-year-old Holsteiner from Germany. He and I practice a lot during the week with my trainer, Amy. I also spend many hours in the barn taking care of Rebel. Knowing your horse well makes it happier and helps it perform better.

My name is Grace Busch. I ride horses in competitions. I learned to ride before I learned to walk, by riding with my dad and by myself. I grew up on a big farm that had many exotic animals. I didn't just ride horses there—I also rode elephants and camels! I have traveled all over the United States, competing in horse shows. Since starting at the age of 9, I've won several grand championships. I also play polo in my hometown of St. Louis, Missouri, at the Kräftig Polo Club.

Rebel and I compete in the hunter class. We are judged on how we look jumping over and riding between fences. We have three attempts each day over a 20-day period. The judges watch our every move. To be at our best, Rebel and I have to work perfectly together. But horses mean more to me than how well they compete. I love them because of their beauty and strength, and I'm thankful for the patience and love they make me feel. Go ahead and pet Rebel if you want. He doesn't bite. Then saddle up with me and jump into this awesome 3D book!

ANIMAL ADVENTURES 3D

BY DAVID E. KLUTHO

CONTENTS CARDS
COLLECT THEM ALL!

52 THE MASCOTS

58 ANIMAL ATHLETES

66 TALE OF THE TAIL

70 THE PREDATORS

76 What are they SAYING?

78 What are they THINKING?

WIDE EYES

Want to see animals up close?
Try binoculars! They not only
make distant objects seem
closer—they let you
see them in 3D.

BINOCULARS

BINOCULARS are really two telescopes that sit side by side. When you look through them, each eye sees the scene from a slightly different angle. The brain combines the information to create a stereoscopic (3D) image. Humans and other animals with two eyes facing forward see objects in 3D. This phenomenon helps us judge the relative distances of nearby objects. If our eyes were farther apart, we could see objects even farther away in 3D.

HOW FAR APART ARE YOUR EYES?
The average distance between human eyes is 2 ½ inches. But a pair of binoculars can increase that distance because the lenses are farther apart!

THE 25¢ TOWER BINOCULARS act as if your eyes were 5 inches apart. This lets you see twice as much depth from a long distance.

Objective lenses (on other side) are a whopping 5 inches apart.

Hand-held BINOCULARS can make the distance between your eyes equal to, smaller than, or wider than 2 ½ inches.

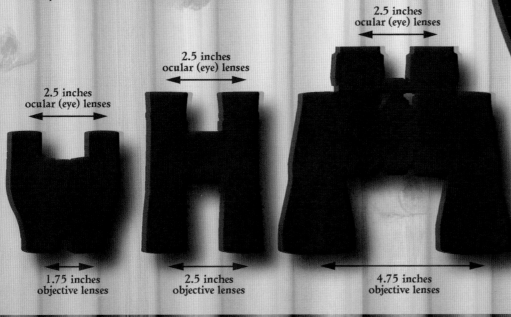

2.5 inches
ocular (eye) lenses

2.5 inches
ocular (eye) lenses

2.5 inches
ocular (eye) lenses

1.75 inches
objective lenses

2.5 inches
objective lenses

4.75 inches
objective lenses

Cool Critters from Around the Globe

Popping out of the page is a green moray eel. This fearsome-looking fish can grow to eight feet and weigh as much as 65 pounds. Prey, such as fish, crabs, and other eels, are no match for the scaleless moray's sharp teeth. Fun fact: The green moray eel has a brown body covered in yellowish mucus. The two colors make the eel look green. The mucus keeps the eel safe from parasites and germs.

FORK IT OVER

Hisss! That forked tongue doesn't have to touch you to sense you. A snake, like this rat snake, can identify prey by its odor. The snake does this by sticking out its tongue to collect another animal's scent molecules. Some snakes use another cool tool to locate a meal. They are able to detect a nearby animal at night by the heat it gives off. Then the snake might spring and swallow its victim whole!

OTTER-LY ADORABLE

Is one cuter than the otter? No, these two African spotted-necked otters are equally adorable! The water-loving mammals hang out in large groups in streams, marshes, and lakes. An otter's sleek body, long tail, waterproof fur, and webbed feet make swimming and diving a cinch. Like humans, these otters like to swim in clear water, where it's easier to spot the catch of the day—fresh fish.

DANGEROUS DRAGON

This is one dragon you can't train! Of the nearly 6,000 species of lizards, the Komodo dragon is the biggest and the baddest. With an average length of nine feet and weight of 200 pounds, Komodos are named for the island Komodo, one of the five islands in Indonesia on which they prowl. These reptiles have long, curved chompers—all the better to tear apart their prey, which could be anything from deer to water buffalo to wild pigs. If an animal it bites gets away, the Komodo follows it, waiting for its meal to die from poison in the Komodo's saliva. Komodos don't breathe fire, but these dragons are still dangerous!

Showstopper

What whiskers! They belong to a California sea lion, a marine mammal native to the Pacific coast of North America. Its sensitive whiskers help it feel for food that swims by. The sleek sea creature can swim up to 25 miles per hour and dive as deep as 1,000 feet on one breath of air to search for a meal. This West Coast wonder is the species most often used in aquatic shows. That's because it is smart and able to move well on land. Fun fact: A group of sea lions that joins together in the water is called a raft.

WHOLE HOG

Camera hog! Actually, the warthog is a lot shier than it looks. This member of the pig family just wants to be left alone to munch on grass and roots, or sit happily in mud to stay cool and escape insects. A native of Africa, the warthog may attack if threatened, using its four sharp tusks. But the warthog prefers to flee from predators, like lions or cheetahs. Able to run at speeds of up to 30 miles an hour, the warthog swerves around like an all-pro running back to avoid becoming a meal. Fun fact: The warthog gets its name from the bumps on the heads of the males. The pads protect it when banging into rivals during the mating season.

SILVER BACK

You've just come face to face with a gorilla. Standing nearly six feet tall and weighing up to 450 pounds, the gorilla is the largest primate. The primate order includes monkeys, apes, and humans. Gorillas stay together in a group called a troop, and each troop's leader is a silverback—an older male gorilla with silver hair on its back. This silverback looks menacing in 3D, but don't be afraid—it's an intelligent, plant-eating, gentle giant.

EARN YOUR STRIPES

What's black and white with stripes all over? The zebra that's looking your way! Zebras are members of the horse family. And speaking of family, the most common zebra species live in groups made up of a male, a few females, and their offspring. Native to Africa, the animals are often on the move, seeking food and water. At night, the male stays awake to keep its family safe from predators like lions and hyenas. Sometimes, families join together to form herds of hundreds or even thousands. If the herd is attacked, family members will protect each other by using their powerful legs to kick the enemy. If that doesn't work, zebras can run as fast as 40 miles per hour!

Stripe Types

Zebra stripes come in handy against predators. They make it difficult for attackers to pick out a single animal. All those moving stripes are confusing! Stripes also make it easier for zebras to identify each other, since no two zebras have the exact same pattern. A baby zebra must quickly recognize its mother's stripes in order to follow her as the herd moves. Although individual zebras have unique stripes, each zebra species shares similar patterns. In one, the stripes are wider and farther apart. Others have some stripes that are more vertical, or have a lighter stripe between the black stripes. The Grant's zebra—shown here—is the smallest type of zebra. At about four feet tall, the Grant's zebra has broad vertical stripes on its trunk, horizontal stripes on its legs and diagonal stripes on its rump. Grant's zebras really believe in togetherness—during the rainy season, as many as 10,000 Grant's zebras might migrate across the African plains in one huge herd!

HORSING AROUND

You can't ride a seahorse! For one thing, they don't make saddles that small. Plus, it's a fish, of course! The seahorse swims in an upright position, pushed forward by teeny-tiny fins on its back that move 35 times a second. Even smaller fins behind the head help it steer. The seahorse is no racehorse. It moves slowly through the water, looking for a piece of sea grass or coral to grip with its tail. Then the seahorse waits for a meal to swim by. Fun fact: The female seahorse passes eggs to the male, which takes care of them in a pouch until they hatch.

16

WATER LION

All hail the lion king—the lionfish king, that is! A cross between a zebra and a nightmare, this small fish packs a potent, painful punch of poison. Its bright, colorful pattern is a warning to predators to steer clear. On its back are up to 18 fins that deliver venom to fish or humans unwise enough to touch it.

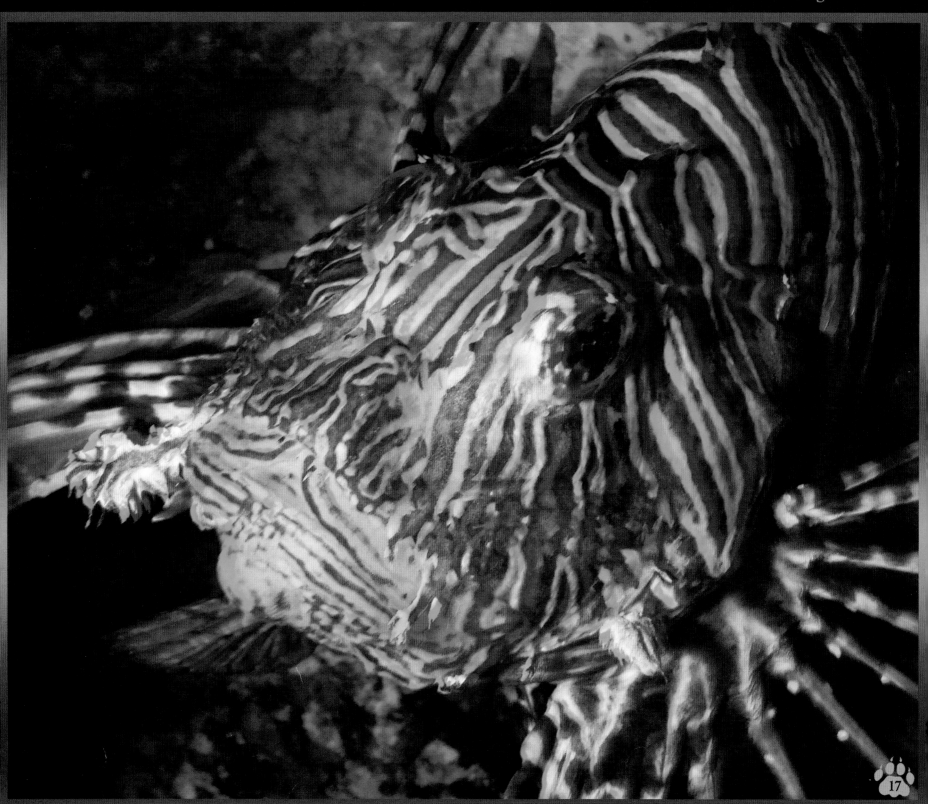

17

This black rhinoceros is the 2D star of this book's cover. Now check it out in full 3D. Those horns look a lot more impressive when they're sticking out of the page! The rhino is even more intimidating in real life, on the grasslands of Africa. There, a riled-up rhino may ram its huge horns into another animal. The humongous front horn can grow as long as five feet! Fun fact: The horns are made of keratin, which is the same substance as our fingernails.

FACES OF THE KINGDOM

From microscopic organisms to whales, scientists have identified about 8.7 million animal species in the world. And there may be as many as 30 million different species. About half of these species are insects. Birds, reptiles, fish, amphibians, and mammals make up only about three percent of all species, but these critters are by far the most photogenic. Here and on the next two pages are some 3D snapshots —but no selfies!—of a few magnificent members of the animal world. Say *cheese!*

He's the mane guy, the top dog (well, cat), king of the jungle, and star of stage and screen—yes, the lion. Okay, lions don't really make their home in a dense jungle—their habitat is the plains and woodland areas of Africa. But this strong, regal face proves that no matter where lions live, they rule.

RED-TAILED HAWK

GIANT ANTEATER

JAGUAR

POLAR BEAR

WILDLIFE Discovery
Learning through INTERACTION

Sea lions are smart and take well to training. That's the reason these lovable marine animals are the stars of the show at the Sea Lion Sound exhibit at the Saint Louis Zoo. In one area of the exhibit, huge pools and a glass-enclosed underwater tunnel allow visitors to view sea lions swimming in a re-creation of their natural habitat. And at the exhibit's First Bank Sea Lion Show, the fish-gobbling mammals show off complicated behaviors in a 40,000-gallon pool. They jump through hoops, walk on their flippers, balance balls on their noses, toss flying discs, and even dance. Audiences love to see these sea lions perform!

PLAY TIME

Every day at the Sea Lion Sound, crowds get to see sea lions being trained. The secret to training a sea lion is something called positive reinforcement. That means when the sea lion does something correctly, such as jump or climb, the trainer gives it fish to eat. The trainer's teaching tool is an object called a target. On page 22, you can see a trainer using a target at the Saint Louis Zoo. If the sea lion follows the target, the trainer might say, "Good," or blow a whistle, then give the animal a fish. Eventually, the sea lion knows what to do when it hears the command or whistle. Sea lions are naturally playful, and for them and their trainers, learning a routine isn't hard work—it's fun!

BACKYARD EXPLORER

NATURE NEARBY

You don't have to live in a jungle to have an animal adventure. A nature explorer can find wildlife everywhere, even in a city park or community garden, or on a tree-lined street. Look up and you'll spot all types of birds in the trees. Look down and you'll notice an entire world of insects at your feet. They may be crawling through grass, hiding under a rock, squirming inside a rotting log, or, like a butterfly, floating in the air. There are 200 million insects for every single person on Earth, so spotting some won't be hard!

You can be a top-notch nature explorer. Just grab a pair of binoculars, a magnifying lens, and a small notebook to jot down what you see. You might see cool living things, such as butterflies (above), pill bugs (far left), and the lubber grasshopper (left). Happy hunting.

LOOK WHO'S IN CAGES NOW

It's a rhino traffic jam! There are about 900 animals in the Lion Country Safari, a drive-through park in Loxahatchee, Florida. These white rhinoceroses are the park's heaviest animals. On the plains of Africa, white rhinos munch grass with their extra-wide mouths. At the park, the 10 usually peaceful rhinos eat about 20 pounds of hay daily. A rhino weighs up to 5,000 pounds, so when a group of rhinos decides to stand in the park's road, cars stop and wait patiently without honking their horns—no one wants to see rhino road rage! Fun fact: A white rhinoceros's tough skin is three inches thick in places. The total weight of the skin is about 1,000 pounds!

AARON'S ANIMAL ADVICE

My name is Aaron Vandeven. I am 8 and in the third grade. At Wild Animal Safari, I got to meet these baby Bengal tigers named Meeko and Binx. The trainer showed me how to hold them by the skin on the backs of their necks. This is how their mother calms them. It is important to remember to have your parent's permission and listen to the animal trainer when you hold exotic animals.

Snakes are my favorite. I have found many in my backyard. Most snakes you find around your house are harmless. If you find one, have a parent or another adult make sure it is okay to get a closer look. A snake expert named Tom brought these snakes to my birthday party. We learned about different types of snakes. He taught us how to hold the snakes with our hands open and to never squeeze. That would scare the snake.

Tom also brought a tarantula. It was very big. Tarantulas are fragile. The spiders can bite, but most types are not dangerous or mean. Tom explained that it's important to learn the proper way to handle different types of animals. It's most important to get an adult's permission before getting close to any animal you don't know.

SNAKE HANDLER

Please touch! That's what Tom Gardner says. He brings his snakes and spiders to kids in hospitals and visits scout troops and birthday parties. These close encounters with exotic animals entertain and educate. Kids learn how the animals feel and behave. Handling animals—with adult supervision—makes you lose your fear of them. You might even come to like animals you once thought were gross!

Giant fern

Ugh! Snakes are slimy and scaly, right? Wrong! If you touched one, you'd know they are dry and smooth. Interacting with animals is a great learning experience. Some of the best places to get up close and personal with critters are zoos and science centers. Many have hands-on programs where you get to hold or feed animals. Safety tip: Always wash your hands after touching an animal.

WEIGHT LIFTERS

Superman has met his match—the leafcutter ant. This amazing ant is a superhero of the insect world. Only one half inch long, the leafcutter ant can carry an object in its mouth that is more than three times its weight. That's like a 100-pound kid lifting and carrying a full-size refrigerator—in his or her mouth! Leafcutter ants live in the rain forests of Central and South America, in colonies of millions. Special types of leafcutter ants called workers cut off chunks of leaves with their super-strong jaws, hold them in their mouths, and take a long hike along the jungle floor back to the nest. No sweat for these mighty insects! The ants don't eat the leaves—they use them to garden! The leaves are turned into an underground compost heap that a fungus grows on. The ants eat the fungus—their reward for hard work!

RECORD BREAKERS

Want to think big? Then consider the African elephant. The colossal pachyderm is the world's largest land animal. The average adult male is 12 feet tall and weighs about 14,000 pounds. That's almost as much as two minivans! Their appetites are also large: They eat up to 300 pounds of food a day and wash it down with 25 gallons of water. Fun fact: Elephant tusks are actually teeth that can grow up to 10 feet long.

LARGE AND IN CHARGE

SOME DANGEROUS ANIMALS

open wide

Say ahh! This mighty mouth belongs to a hippopotamus, one of the most fearsome animals in the world. It spends most of its time cooling off in rivers, eating fruits and veggies, and minding its own business. But don't get it angry: Those upper and lower teeth can grow as long as 20 inches. And the hippo will use them to spear anything that bothers it—including people.

WARNING!

cute but nasty

Danger! Poison dart frogs are tiny, toxic terrors. The skin of some species contains a chemical so deadly that it can sicken or kill any animal that touches or eats it. The amount of this poison that would fit on the period at the end of this sentence could kill a person. The frogs' bright colors warn predators to keep away, allowing the frogs to fearlessly hop around in the rain forests of Central and South America. Fun fact: Some native tribes rub the frogs' poison onto darts to use as weapons.

High, guy! In this book, you and a giraffe can see eye to eye. In a zoo, you might need a very tall ladder to do that. The giraffe is the tallest land animal in the world. A male can reach up to 18 feet in height, with six-foot-long legs and an equally long 600-pound neck. All this length, plus a one-and-a-half-foot-long tongue, helps a giraffe snack on leaves in tall trees. Giraffes often show affection by touching their necks together. Young giraffes may play fight by banging necks (below left). Older giraffes sometimes fight this way more seriously, to prove who's boss.

WORLD SPEED records

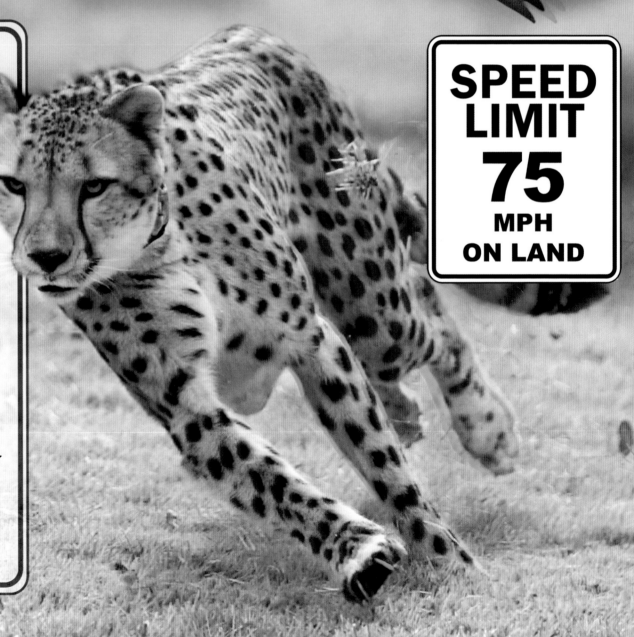

SPEED LIMIT 200 MPH IN THE AIR

SPEED LIMIT 75 MPH ON LAND

The Flash! If speed thrills, then the cheetah is the most thrilling. The world's fastest land animal, this big cat can reach a speed of 60 miles per hour in three seconds and has a top speed of nearly 70 miles per hour—almost three times faster than the fastest human sprinter. The speed demon's secret? Long legs, a flexible spine, claws that grip the ground, and the ability to cover about 21 feet in one stride.

Winged Wonder! The swiftest bird of prey is the falcon, and the speediest falcon is the peregrine—thanks to its slim body, pointed wings, and narrow tail. The peregrine flies above its prey, then dive bombs toward it at speeds of up to 200 miles per hour, making it the fastest animal of all.

SLOW DOWN

The animal world has its share of slowpokes, and the slowest may be the snail. It slimes along at less than one inch per minute. Though quicker, the sloth is no ball of energy. It spends most of its time hanging upside down in trees. Like a couch potato, it hardly moves, and when it does, it takes about one minute to cover eight feet. The giant tortoise is a little faster but still no speedster. It moves at less than one-fifth of a mile per hour and would take about an hour to walk one city block. But you might too, if you had to carry a giant shell on your back!

SLOW
XING

CIRCUS ANIMALS

The *Ringling Bros.* and *Barnum & Bailey*™ circus is famous for its clowns and acrobats, but for many people, its performing animals are the main attraction. One of *Ringling Bros.'* three circuses tours with 85 animals—from elephants and tigers to pigs, goats, and kangaroos. They are a big reason this circus is called The Greatest Show On Earth.

AMAZING ANIMALS
Steal the Show

THE GREATEST SHOW ON EARTH™

They're really horsing around. The Thundering Cossack Warriors perform breathtaking feats on spectacular steeds. In one maneuver, five people form a human pyramid on top of two horses galloping at 25 miles per hour!

Trainer Alexander Lacey trusts these big cats with his life! A tiger, for example, can kill with a single bite (yikes!). Lacey has helped raise Bengal tigers, lions, and leopards from birth, so for him, they're part of the family. He can identify individual cats by their roars and their different personalities: One likes to play in the water, while another is mischievous.

Lacey takes good care of his cats. He gets up at 6:30 in the morning to give them water and have them practice their routines. Lacey watches each cat to see how he can work its natural behavior into the act. Then it's time for breakfast! Each cat eats up to 16 pounds of meat every day. Later, the cats get to play with branches, balls, and water basins. At night, the sleepy cats get to lap up warm milk and liver oil to keep their coats healthy and shiny.

Lacey commands his cats in both English and German. But it's mostly Lacey's close bond with the beautiful beasts that makes it possible for him to show off their awesome strength and agility—and have them stand tall.

Check out the leg work! Elephants not only demonstrate brains and good balance at the circus, but they also show off their artistic skills. A few of the Asian elephants enjoy taking a paintbrush to canvas. At each show, paintings made by these pachyderm Picassos—like the one above—are given away to audience members.

CIRCUS DOG

Hans Klose is a dog's best friend. The *Ringling Bros.* trainer has 21 canines that he cares for as if they were his children. He rescued most of them from pounds and shelters. His closeness with his dogs makes it easy to train them to jump rope, do somersaults, stand on two legs, and go down a slide. One little dog named Twiggy puts on a show by jumping off a 16-foot-high platform and into Klose's waiting arms. "It even sits on my shoulder like a parrot," says Klose. What are the cute canines' favorite reward? Hot dogs!

"Don't muss my feathers!" Everything about the grey-crowned crane, which lives in Africa, is fabulous—from its golden plumage and black and white wings to the red pouch on its neck. Other crane species are jealous!

FASHION PARADE

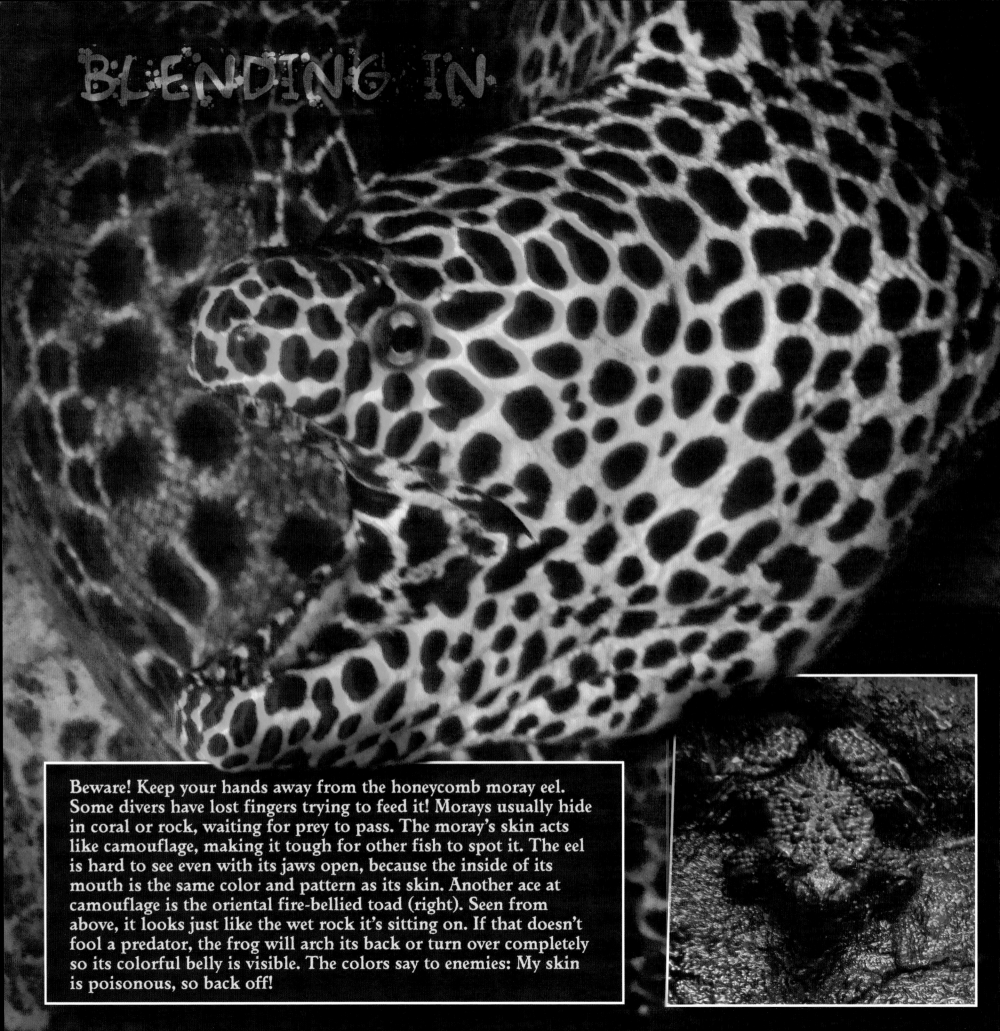

BLENDING IN

Beware! Keep your hands away from the honeycomb moray eel. Some divers have lost fingers trying to feed it! Morays usually hide in coral or rock, waiting for prey to pass. The moray's skin acts like camouflage, making it tough for other fish to spot it. The eel is hard to see even with its jaws open, because the inside of its mouth is the same color and pattern as its skin. Another ace at camouflage is the oriental fire-bellied toad (right). Seen from above, it looks just like the wet rock it's sitting on. If that doesn't fool a predator, the frog will arch its back or turn over completely so its colorful belly is visible. The colors say to enemies: My skin is poisonous, so back off!

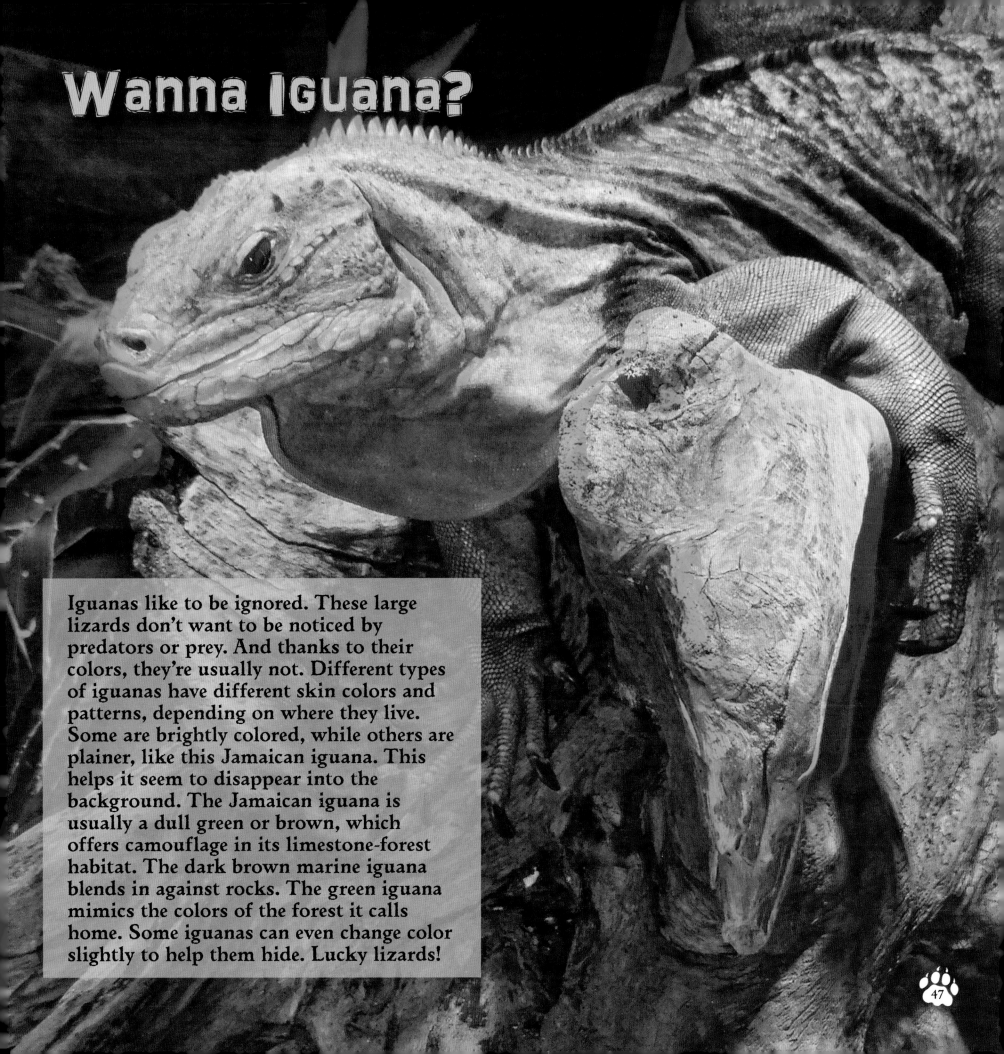

Wanna Iguana?

Iguanas like to be ignored. These large lizards don't want to be noticed by predators or prey. And thanks to their colors, they're usually not. Different types of iguanas have different skin colors and patterns, depending on where they live. Some are brightly colored, while others are plainer, like this Jamaican iguana. This helps it seem to disappear into the background. The Jamaican iguana is usually a dull green or brown, which offers camouflage in its limestone-forest habitat. The dark brown marine iguana blends in against rocks. The green iguana mimics the colors of the forest it calls home. Some iguanas can even change color slightly to help them hide. Lucky lizards!

Audiences at the Miami Seaquarium flip out when this orca does a backflip. Lolita the orca, or killer whale, is one of the top attractions at the marine-life entertainment park. The largest member of the dolphin family, orcas can grow to be 33 feet long and weigh as much as nine tons. When the orca leaps out of the water, it makes a monster splash, like the world's biggest cannonball. Lolita is one killer performer!

SPLISHY SPLASHY WATER FUN

Flying off the page are some frisky bottlenose dolphins performing at the Miami Seaquarium. This is where the popular TV show *Flipper* was filmed. Brainy, graceful, and playful, dolphins are masters at doing tricks, such as dancing upright along the water's surface on their tails, leaping in formation, and generally acting like Olympic synchronized swimmers. California sea lions (right) are also aquatic athletes. At the Miami Seaquarium, these amazing mammals walk on their flippers, jump through hoops, and climb stairs.

DISC DOGS

Bow-WOW! The best pass-catchers in football have nothing on Jazmin, a 5-year-old Australian shepherd. Jazmin is a member of the St. Louis Disc Dog club. The group teaches owners how to get their dogs started in the sport of disc-catching. To take part, you only need a dog and a disc. First, get the dog used to the disc: Use it as a water bowl and play tug games with it. Take out the disc only when it's time to play, so your dog will be excited to see it. Then start rolling the disc along the ground, so Fido gets practice grabbing a spinning disc. Next, make short tosses to the dog, almost flipping the disc at its mouth. Then slowly increase the distance of the tosses. It takes time and patience to teach your dog. The payoff? You and your pet will have even more fun together.

DO NOT PUT YOUR FINGER IN HIS MOUTH

BEWARE OF THE DOG

FREEDOM
THE AMERICAN BALD EAGLE

It's America's mascot! The bald eagle has been the national bird of the United States since 1782. This majestic bald eagle, named Freedom, lives at the World Bird Sanctuary, a nature park founded in Missouri by bird researcher Walter Crawford Jr. There, Crawford and his staff rescue, care for, and provide homes to injured birds, especially birds of prey such as eagles and owls. Many of the birds are trained to soar at events and demonstrations around the country, to help educate people about our feathered friends. The fantastic Freedom has circled stadiums at professional baseball and football games during the national anthem. This bird definitely has the flight stuff! Read about other animal mascots on the next few pages.

THE MASCOTS

Hi, I'm Butler Blue III, but you can call me Trip. That's short for Triple, because I'm the third English bulldog mascot for Butler University, in Indianapolis, Indiana. As the school mascot, I have a lot of duties. You can find me posing for photos, cruising in my own car (the Blue Mobile), and attending lots of big events. There's also a children's book all about me, because I'm so cute! I even have my own social media accounts. But what I like best is appearing at Butler basketball games. Nothing gets me more excited than the sight of a basketball. I may not be great at dribbling, but I'm pretty good at drooling!

BLUE III
BUTLER
UNIVERSITY

Let's go, tigers! From the Detroit Tigers to the Cincinnati Bengals to the Hamilton Tiger-Cats (of the Canadian Football League), sports teams love to name themselves after the largest, most powerful cat in the world. As long as nine feet and weighing up to 660 pounds, tigers are fierce, stealthy hunters. They will attack prey four times their own size, including elephants. Tigers are able to swim and have been known to kill crocodiles. There are six tiger subspecies in the world, and their total population is only around 3,200. At the beginning of the 20th century, there were about 100,000 tigers. The tiger may be an endangered species, but it isn't endangered as a mascot: The sports teams of twelve Division One universities are known as the tigers. Here are the schools whose mascots roar:

Auburn University,
Auburn, Alabama
Clemson University,
Clemson, South Carolina
Jackson State University,
Jackson, Mississippi
Louisiana State University,
Baton Rouge, Louisiana
University of Memphis,
Memphis, Tennessee
University of Missouri,
Columbia, Missouri
University of the Pacific,
Stockton, California
Princeton University,
Princeton, New Jersey
Savannah State University,
Savannah, Georgia
Tennessee State University,
Nashville, Tennessee
Texas Southern University,
Houston, Texas

BULL HORNS

Where does this buffalo roam? At the University of Colorado, in Boulder. Ralphie the Buffalo (below) is the mascot for the school's sports teams. When Ralphie leads Colorado's football team onto the field before the start and second half of every home game, even the opposing team stops and watches the thundering behemoth. A female buffalo (it's really a bison), Ralphie weighs around 1,000 pounds, can run 25 miles per hour, and needs five handlers to control it.

The mascot of the University of Texas at Austin is a Texas Longhorn named Bevo (right). A Longhorn has really long horns: They can measure seven feet from tip to tip. The school likes to find steers that are orange and white, because those are the sports teams' colors. When Bevo is on the sidelines at home football games, it's best to steer clear of the 2,000-pound steer!

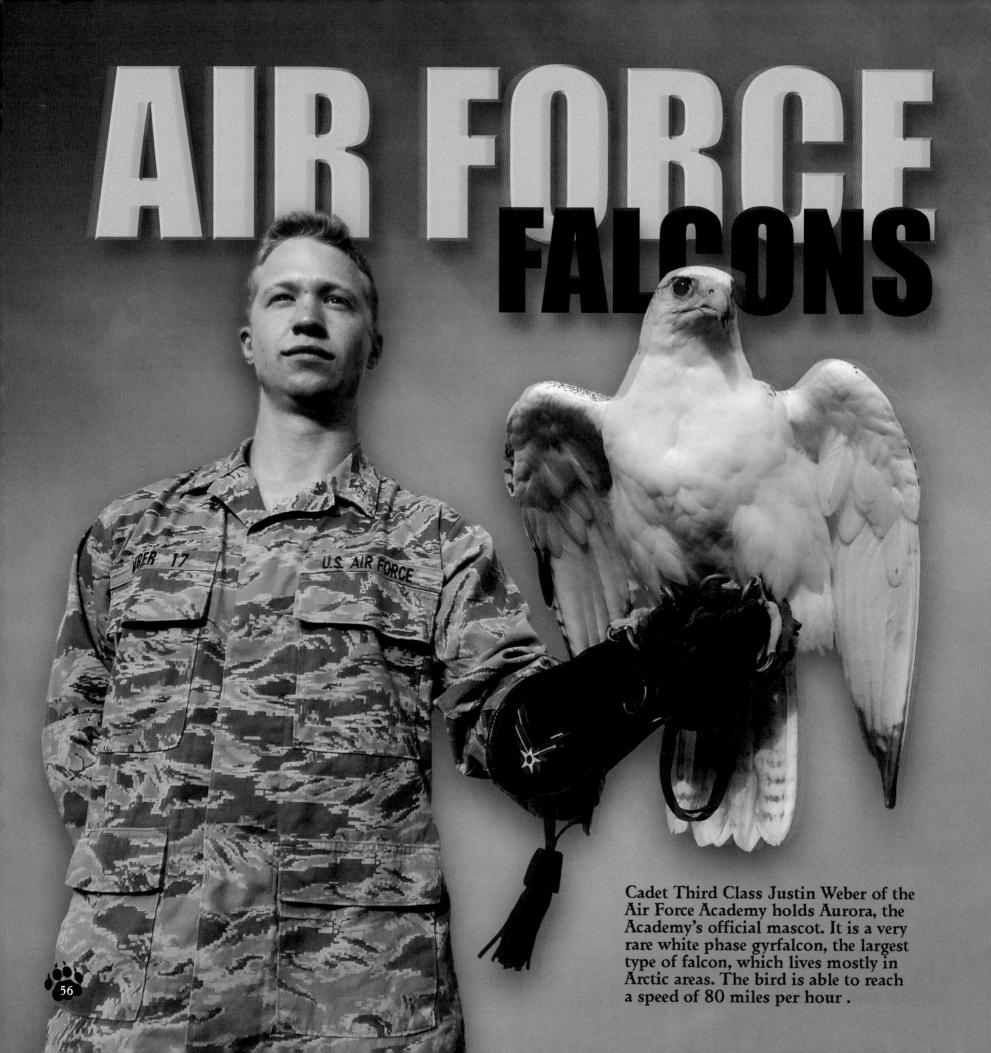

AIR FORCE FALCONS

Cadet Third Class Justin Weber of the Air Force Academy holds Aurora, the Academy's official mascot. It is a very rare white phase gyrfalcon, the largest type of falcon, which lives mostly in Arctic areas. The bird is able to reach a speed of 80 miles per hour .

LIVE AIR POWER

What do a falcon and an Air Force pilot have in common? They fly fast, maneuver gracefully, are fearless, have sharp eyesight (a falcon's eyesight is eight times sharper than a human's), and are alert. Ace (right), a large, powerful gyr-saker falcon, is one of nearly a dozen mascot falcons trained by the Cadet Falconry Team. Ace flies at halftime of the Air Force Academy's home football games, where it chases a lure whirled around by a cadet at the 50-yard line. When it catches it in its talons, Ace gets its meal for the day—and the cheers of 40,000 fans in the stands. Score one for the falcon!

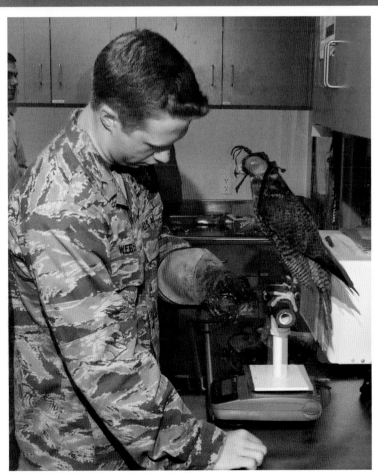

Cadet Weber learns about Ace's health by weighing the falcon. The black airplane next to Ace is the U.S. Air Force's B-2 Spirit. This supersonic "flying wing" looks a lot like Ace's tail feathers.

57

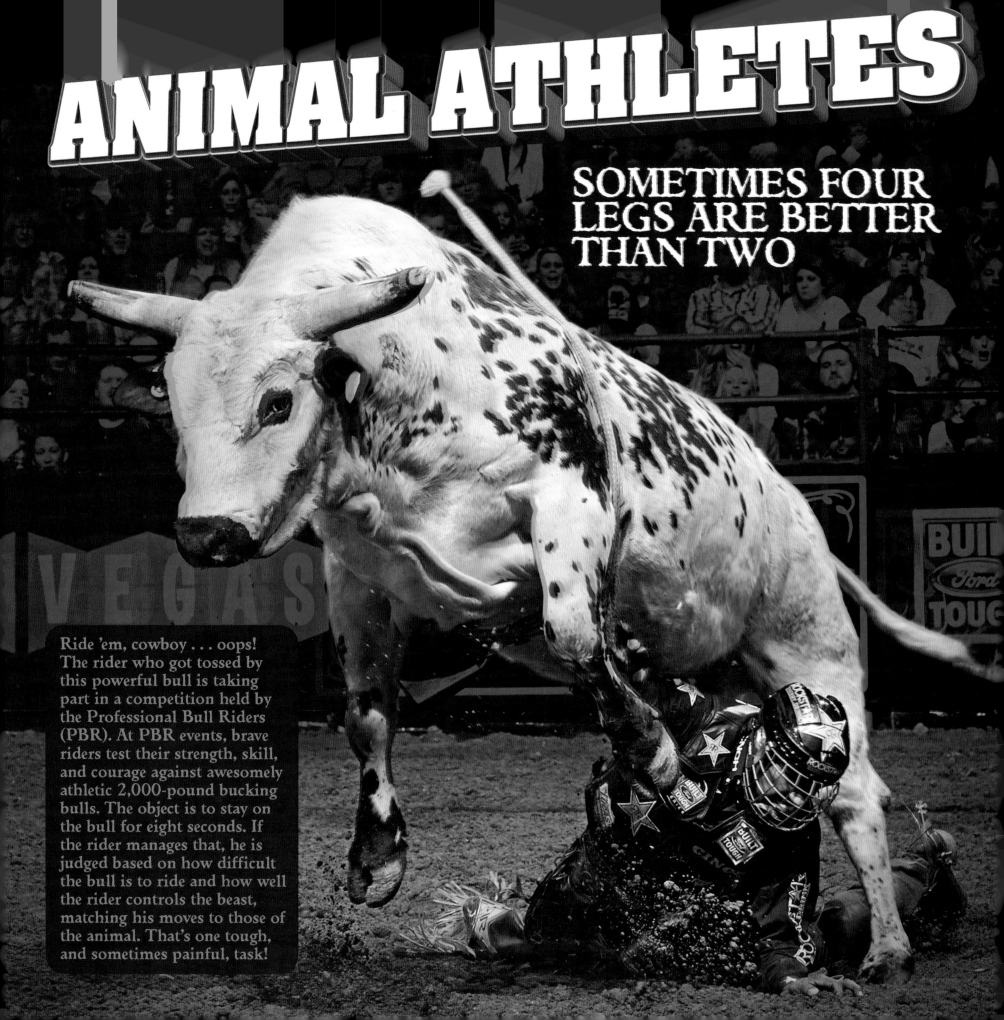

ANIMAL ATHLETES

SOMETIMES FOUR LEGS ARE BETTER THAN TWO

Ride 'em, cowboy . . . oops! The rider who got tossed by this powerful bull is taking part in a competition held by the Professional Bull Riders (PBR). At PBR events, brave riders test their strength, skill, and courage against awesomely athletic 2,000-pound bucking bulls. The object is to stay on the bull for eight seconds. If the rider manages that, he is judged based on how difficult the bull is to ride and how well the rider controls the beast, matching his moves to those of the animal. That's one tough, and sometimes painful, task!

Rough Ride

A bull rider holds a rope that circles the bull behind its front legs. If the rider lets go of the rope, his free hand touches the bull or himself, or he touches the ground, he's disqualified. Riders often wear either a traditional cowboy hat or a helmet with a face shield to protect their heads. They also must wear a protective vest to prevent injuries caused by the bull's hooves and horns.

The photos on this page show the bull rider being thrown from the bull from two different angles. The photo at the top shows the scene from above. The photo at the bottom gives an eye-level view of the same moment. Either way you look at it, this rider is about to hit the ground hard!

Talk about fast food! The annual National Championship Chuckwagon Race takes place over three days in Clinton, Arkansas. Chuckwagons are kitchens on wheels. They were used to feed cowboys on cattle drives. To celebrate those times, more than 300 mules and horses pull 150 chuckwagon teams. The object of the race: to get the fastest time over a course that's as long as half a mile. Each wagon has a three-person team: a driver, a person inside the wagon, and a horseman who rides alongside the wagon. Contestants come from all over the U. S. and from as far away as New Zealand. Winning wagons get a share in the more than $25,000 in prizes and prize money. That could buy a lot of chow!

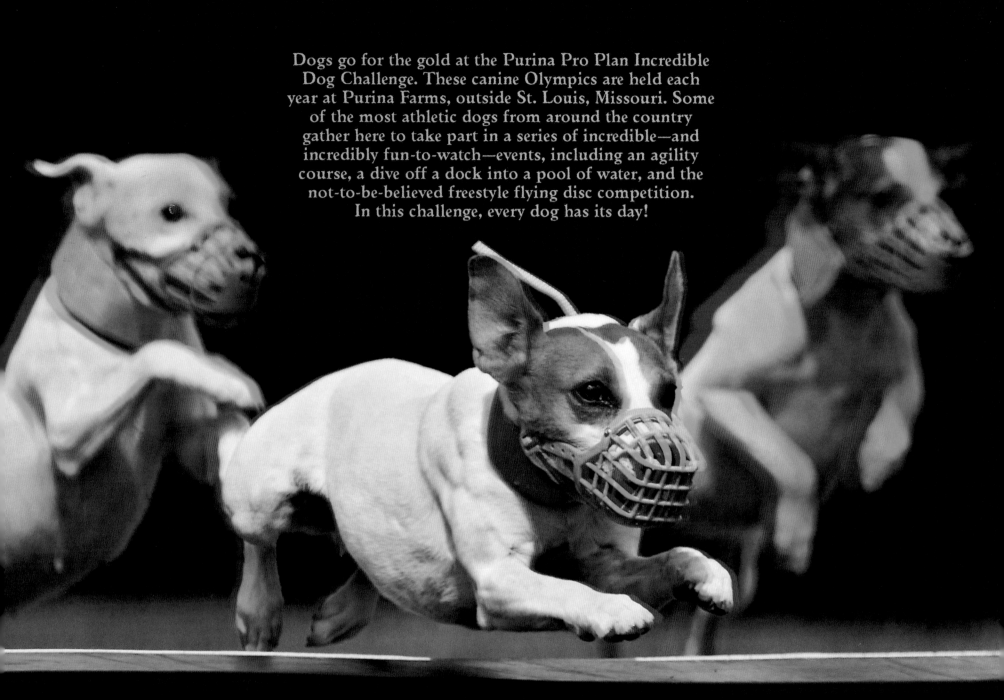

Dogs go for the gold at the Purina Pro Plan Incredible Dog Challenge. These canine Olympics are held each year at Purina Farms, outside St. Louis, Missouri. Some of the most athletic dogs from around the country gather here to take part in a series of incredible—and incredibly fun-to-watch—events, including an agility course, a dive off a dock into a pool of water, and the not-to-be-believed freestyle flying disc competition. In this challenge, every dog has its day!

PURINA®
PRO PLAN®
INCREDIBLE DOG
Challenge®

Paw power! The trio of canines on page 62 is taking part in the Jack Russell Terriers Hurdle Race—a competition in which the pooches must leap over hurdles. The fleet four-footers are, from left to right, Scout, a 5-year-old male, Dinan, an 8-year-old female, and Meme, a 5-year-old female. Shown on this page is one of the coolest events: the Incredible Fetch. Dogs leap into a pool, trying to knock down a bumper that dangles over the water. The dog that reaches the bumper from the farthest distance wins.

He's pretty mouthy! Cowboy, a 5-year-old Chesapeake Bay retriever, showed off his skill and strength at the Incredible Fetch event. Cowboy took first place with a giant jump of 23 feet, six inches. Now that's how to make a big splash!

63

TOP DOGS

Kate is jumping for joy! The 4-year-old border collie leaps over a hurdle during the Large-Dog Agility event. Pooches must race through a course that includes tunnels, slalom gates, and climbing boards. In the small photo, Paddy, another 4-year-old border collie, competes in the 30-Weave-Pole Up-and-Back event. Dogs race to see which is fastest at maneuvering between a total of 60 poles without missing one. Competitors surely end up dog-tired!

PLAYFUL PUPS

This duo has a leg up on the competition. In the Freestyle Flying Disc competition, dogs and trainers perform unbelievable routines set to music. Pairs are judged on the catches the dog makes, the creativity and originality of the routine, and how well they make use of the entire field. The winner of this event, Riley, a 3-year-old border collie, balances on the foot of its trainer, Mark Faragoi of Plainfield, Illinois. (Inset) Laika, a 4-year-old Belgian Malinois, jumps over the knee of owner Mona Konishi of Ohtsu, Shiga, Japan, to catch the disc in midair.
Doggone incredible!

A TALE OF THE TAIL

Not Just for WAGGING

The red-panda's tail is un-fur-gettable! This little creature is only about three feet long, and 18 inches of that is its thick tail. The red panda spends most of its life in trees in the mountain areas of Asia, sleeping, breeding, and searching for bamboo, fruit, and insects to eat. Roaming from branch to branch, the red panda uses its tail to balance. When winter comes, the animal wraps that soft, furry tail around itself like a colorful blanket to stay warm. That's what we call bright-eyed and bushy-tailed!

THAT'S A WRAP

The chameleon is famous for changing the color of its skin at will. But this four-horned chameleon, like the more than 100 other chameleon species, can also move each eye separately, shoot out its sticky tongue to catch insects, grip branches with its fingers and toes, and use its terrific tail like a hand. The tail is prehensile, which means it can curl and wrap around branches. All these traits make living in trees a snap. Color us impressed! Fun fact: A chameleon's tongue can be longer than its body.

SPINE DESIGN

Think the African crested porcupine is prickly? Quill-ty as charged! This rodent's sharp quills can grow to be 14 inches. It uses them to defend itself against anything from a lion to a bird of prey. The porcupine gives a warning by raising its quills, then shakes the tail quills to make them rattle. The next step is to run backward, slamming the quills against the attacker. The quills are pulled out of the porcupine's back as they stick into the enemy's skin. Talk about being well armed—rather, well backed! Fun fact: This is the largest rodent in Africa.

SUPER-SIZE TAIL

This whopper of a tail belongs to a killer whale. Also called orcas, killer whales roam the oceans in groups, like packs of wolves. They eat anything they can find, from sharks to walruses to other whales. Their broad tails help them zip through the water at speeds of up to 35 miles per hour. They also use their tails to slap the surface of the water, making waves that knock penguins and sea lions off ice floes. Then orcas have a whale of a time feeding on their prey.

The vinegaroon has one of nature's tiniest tails. Related to spiders and scorpions, these arachnids whip their mini-tail back and forth to feel what's nearby. The vinegaroon gets its name from a stinging acid, which smells like vinegar, that it sprays in self-defense.

mini tail

PREDATORS
NATURE'S EXPERT HUNTERS

CROC ON!

It's lunchtime, and a blue wildebeest is this crocodile's main course. The wildebeest is a large antelope that lives in Africa. This one made the mistake of crossing a river where a crocodile lurked. Crocs use keen senses of hearing and eyesight to search for prey. Since a croc can bite, but not chew, it clamps the beast in its viselike jaws and pulls it under, twisting the poor victim around to tear off pieces. The raging reptile stores the body underwater for later meals.

GREAT GRIZZLIES

Pay attention to these bear facts: No human can outrun a bear, so don't disturb one, especially near its cubs or food. Bears are the largest meat-eating land animals, and among the fiercest is the grizzly, a type of brown bear that can grow to almost 10 feet tall and weigh a ton. Though they often eat plants, grizzlies also use their sharp teeth and long claws to kill large mammals, including other bears. Those built-in weapons help the grizzly pull salmon, a tasty treat, out of streams. The grizzly's scientific name is *Ursus arctos horribilis*, and running into one can definitely be a horrible experience.

MOUNTAIN MANEUVER

Cougars go by many different names—mountain lion, puma, and panther to name a few. But if you're a bighorn sheep, this big cat spells one thing—trouble! A cougar can bring down an animal much larger than itself. A cougar's legs are so strong, it can leap 20 feet up or down a cliff to catch prey. After the cougar trips its fleeing victim with an outstretched paw, it holds down the prey with its claws and kills it with a bite.

ATTACK FROM BEHIND!

It's a big-cat attack! Cougars silently stalk an animal and then pounce, using an amazing burst of speed. This fantastic feline has grabbed a mule deer by the neck. Fun fact: Cougars have the largest range of any land mammal in the western hemisphere—from Canada to Argentina.

PEARLY WHITES

Even a photo of a shark is pretty scary. For hundreds of millions of years, sharks have been the great hunters of the sea, tearing apart prey with their rows of sharp, pointed teeth. These predators locate food at a distance using their incredible sense of smell and eyes that see in dim light. Sharks can also feel vibrations in the water and sense electrical fields produced by other fish. Sharks are deadly dudes!

NOSE HOSE

No need to be afraid of a giant anteater...unless you're an ant! This native of South and Central America doesn't even have teeth. The furry mammal does have four-inch-long claws that it uses to rip a hole in an anthill or a termite mound. The anteater sticks its big schnoz into the colony and starts slurping insects with its sticky two-foot-long tongue. It can eat as many as 35,000 ants and termites in a day.
Ant that amazing!